BY BUIHE MADU

HEROmanity: 24 Hours to a HEROic Life

The 24 Hour Blueprint: Secrets of Lifestyle Design and Time Management Planner

24 HOUR BLUEPRINT: LIFESTYLE DESIGN & TIME MANAGEMENT PLAYBOOK

24 HOUR BLUEPRINT

LIFESTYLE DESIGN & TIME MANAGEMENT PLAYBOOK

BUIHE
MADU

You are here.

Robson and Puritan, LLC

P.O. Box 1107
Houston, TX 77410

Published in the United States by Robson and Puritan, LLC

ISBN: 979-8-9895548-0-5

THIS PAGE INTENTIONALLY LEFT BLANK

TABLE OF [INTENT]IONS

THIS PAGE INTENTIONALLY LEFT BLANK

FOREWORD

To the Courageous Action Taker:

Thank you for purchasing your 24 Hour Blueprint Program.

Now, imagine having a Genie's lamp with 3 wishes...

But - plot twist, you could make as many wishes as you needed to make under one condition. And that condition is that you can continue making wishes as long as you keep the lamp polished. Now, how polished would you keep the lamp?

I'd hope VERY polished is your answer. And so it is with the skills you'll be polishing as a result of using this playbook to design the parts of your life that your wishes have not yet come true in.

This program is designed to do one thing and one thing only – clear your mind of the millions of possible distractions modern life throws your way and give you access to your most precious asset, your mind. I personally believe that the clearer we are and the better we are at managing the tasks, events and duties of life that are cyclical in nature, the happier we become. The happier we become, the greater the level of freedom and peace we experience to express ourselves, share our ideas and creative potential with others. This is primarily because of a newfound sense of control of our life. When this happens, we get a taste of the deeper parts of ourselves that consist of a heroic nature and our humanity. And when this happens, we tap into our HEROmanity, the part of us that has both the courage and compassion to give our gifts to the world unapologetically.

I hope by applying the exercises in this playbook that you will cultivate the practices required for to experience your genie like powers of your HEROmanity and share it with the world.

Sincerely,

Buihe Madu

Buihe Madu & Co.

THIS PAGE INTENTIONALLY LEFT BLANK

ACKNOWLEDGMENTS

 I can't recall who uttered the quote "no man is an island." Whoever it was, was absolutely right. What you have in your hands is a product of decades of mentoring, coaching, schooling and conversing with some of the greatest minds that have ever lived. It may sound like an exaggeration, but it's not.

Every mind we encounter is tethered to an eternal chain of ideas that goes back to the beginning of human history. Therefore, no conversation that I've had about my life, the future and its visions has been in a vacuum.

This edition of the 24 Hour Blueprint comes as a result of entering a particular phase of my life where I've seen the impact and results of the coaching inspired by the methodology. And I'm even more convinced today that more students, business professionals, moms, dads, entrepreneurs and business owners alike can truly reap great benefits in their lives by applying its principles and concepts.

Some of the friends, associates and entities that I'd like to credit for my confidence in the relevance of the 24 Hour Blueprint's approach to lifestyle design today include:

Dr. Analeena Parhankangas, from The University of Illinois Chicago's Business School for letting me guest lecture and share 24 Hour Blueprint collaborative initiatives with her students

The International Council for Open and Distance Education Conference (ICDE) for accepting a joint proposal to present at their international conference to share the implications of 24 Hour Blueprint case studies on the on student retention and success rates when blended with learning management system platforms.

Kofi Marfo, who reminds me that he's forever going to look at his life with a 5-Kingdom based approach

Mr. Brock for telling me this summer to think BIGGER and follow through on the blueprint I've created or face the consequences of living a life of struggle and regret.

And lastly, Maya "Bear" Bechi who's been a great 24 Hour Blueprint method student-practitioner as well as a super cheerleader of my efforts to resuscitate parts of the work that I'd overlooked and maybe even underestimated.

There are countless others who were included in the previous edition's foreword and in the interest of saving time and space, I've created a page on my blog for them **here**. You can also visit **buihemadu.com/ acknowledgements**.

And lastly, I will forever have to extend a special thanks to the State University of New York at Buffalo and Shanna Crump-Owens, the Director of the Collegiate Science & Technology Entry Program for providing me with an academic environment to empower the next generation of scientists, engineers and inventors with the 24 Hour Blueprint program that will not only impact them directly but spill into the lives of those whose lives they touch.

With all my he[Art],

Buihe Madu

Founder | 24 Hour Blueprint Academy

WARNING: DO NOT TRY THIS AT HOME UNLESS...

You want a **personal transformation**. I remember the morning in the hotel common area where I sat for a continental breakfast trying to eat a muffin and drink juice. Chewing and swallowing was so painful. After spending three days and nights in a hotel room with no food or water, my body had to adjust to eating again especially my throat. What happened? That's another story. And I'm happy to say I wrote a book about it. More on that later. But what happened in those 3 days and nights in a hotel on the border of Northwest Indiana and Illinois, February 2011, is where this breakthrough work you are reading was channeled from. I was at the end of a life I didn't want to live anymore. To put it bluntly, I wanted to end it. But I didn't know the best way to do it without bringing on pain to my body. So, the best thing I could do was withdraw from the world as I knew it – I withdrew from a wife and two children, friends, money, and what I knew then as my home. I shut out the world. I went inward to explore the person I'd grown to hate. In the end, I came out from the experience ready to live a transformed life.

But **how could I guarantee** that this new life was going to be different and distinct from the previous one that I'd lived up to that point? I knew the answer was in designing a life that inspired me based on love, generosity and acceptance, and I knew taking actions that were aligned with that design would be required. The ease and flow that my life possessed after coming out of that hotel was miraculous. The secrets I learned about how to create that life of flow, ease and peace of mind is what I am giving you access to discover and create for yourself in this book. If you're ridiculously exhausted from the "Ok, this time I'm going to really change…" yo-yo or want a future that you feel you can create and control; this playbook is EXACTLY one of the tools that you'll need on that journey.

Before **moving ahead**, there's one question that you have to answer – well perhaps a few questions.

What is your ideal lifestyle and are you living it? Are you taking steps towards it daily? What system(s) do you have in place to support you? Why does it matter to you that you design your life and live it without the drama? Are you ready, willing and able to do whatever it takes to create a life based on your LifeStyle blueprint? If so, continue reading and commit to participating as a case study member until you gain mastery of the methodology presented.

The cart before the 24 Hour Blueprint Horse - In my first book HEROmanity: 24 Hour to a HEROic Life[1], I acknowledge that we live in hyper-accelerated times that leave many stranded and stressed as the new economy unfolds. Also that, collectively, we are all desperately in need of HEROic solutions to this dilemma. This book is one of those types of solutions. And in order to get the value of such a solution, I'd like to take a moment to define what is meant by LifeStyle Design. LifeStyle design is the process of looking at all of the activities of one's life, capturing its predictable trends in major areas such as faith, relationships, money, emotions and fitness, and using technology to create, automate, and integrate that life so that it flows and floats you towards your most meaningful goals. If this sounds remotely exciting to you - you're in the right place at the right time. And you can start today with this blueprint by creating a life of "right times". Welcome home.

---

1   Get a free copy at buihemadu.com/heromanitybook

HOW TO USE THIS PLAYBOOK

This playbook is designed to be reusable for as long as you need to use it. There are templates that you can print and reuse over and over again. Just as the Karate Kid had to sand the floor and paint the fence over and over again, you can use this playbook to do your set of exercises that will guarantee you victory in your academic, professional and entrepreneurial battles when the pressure is on. But it will only happen by rigorous, undying, unrelenting practice.

It's been written to be easy to read, easy to follow and easy to see results from. The digital worksheets that correspond with this playbook are where the magic lives. In our digital era, writing something down and doing the hand calculations to score your results is not as appetizing as it once was. So, I've designed and customized some templates that will allow the users of this playbook to easily integrate this program into whatever tools they're already using to leverage their time.

Consciousness and Productivity

One last thing - Before you get too far, I want to be clear about what it'll take for you to get the best results from using this playbook. And it comes down to one word - Courage. Courage is a fundamental state of being and level of consciousness you'll need to get the most out of this playbook. This occured to me when I realized our levels of consciousness impact our productivity. For example, if you're a procrastinator, trying to stop the behavior isn't just a matter of getting a better planner or downloading the latest productivity app. Sometimes doing what you've been putting off for years or perhaps have not done before requires addressing fears and your lack of courage first. But if you don't see that connection, you'll likely keep scratching your head for solutions while searching for external tools vs. Using your schedule to address what you're afraid of that's justifying the behavior.

So with that, I'll close with a favorite quote of mine:

> "A sword is useless in the hands of a coward."
>
> - Nichiren Daishonin, Buddhist Monk

This playbook is essentially a sword for productivity. And you can cut through years of procrastination within days, sometimes hours or even minutes by using it. But this will not happen if you lack courage when it's time for making key decisions and take action accordingly.

So what do you do when you don't have courage? Or what if you already have courage and you need something more to help you in your situation? To help with these questions, I've borrowed the Buddhist's Ten Worlds of the Human Condition model to help you identify where you are on any given day and select the best state of consciousness that will help you take the actions that are right for you.

As you take actions inspired by this playbook and in your life, you can use the table below to self assess and identify what state(s) of mind you are stopping you and which one will support you with getting the results you wish to produce most.

The Ten Worlds of the Human Condition		
No.	**World**	**Characterized by**
10	Buddhahood	**Wisdom, compassion, courage, life force which illuminates the positive aspects of each of the other nine worlds.**
9	Bodhisattva*	Compassion or acting selflessly for other people, without expecting a reward.
8	Realization	Gaining wisdom and insight through the effects of learning and by observing the world.
7	Learning	Awakening to impermanence. Striving for self-improvement from learning new concepts through studying the teachings of others. This is the basis for realization.
6	Rapture, or Heaven	Fleeting happiness. Intense pleasure and happiness resulting from the joy of having one's desires fulfilled; heightened awareness and feeling glad to be alive.
5	Humanity, or Tranquility	Being at peace and in control of desires; ability to act with reason and humanity.
4	Anger	Strong tendency to compare oneself with and a preoccupation with surpassing others. Hippocrisy and betrayal. Passion to fight injustice and create a better world; becoming a creative force for change.
3	Animality	Motivation based on immediate gain or loss rather than on reason or logic. Baseness and cruelty, such as seen in wartime. The normal instinct to survive (sleep, eat, make love) and to protect and nurture life.
2	Hunger	The inability to use desires creatively and or becoming slaves to them and suffering as a result. The desire to live and achieve goals; yearning to improve things for yourself and others. Desires and wants can provide impetus for self improvement, for human advancement.
1	Hell	The feeling that living itself is suffering and that whatever one sees or encounters causes more suffering. Being controlled by destructive impulses. Really understanding what the state of hell feels like can lead to the desire and wisdom to help others.

Source & Credits: SGI USA

*Bodhisattva: The word consists of bodhi (enlightenment) and sattva (beings) and means someone who seeks enlightenment for themselves and others.

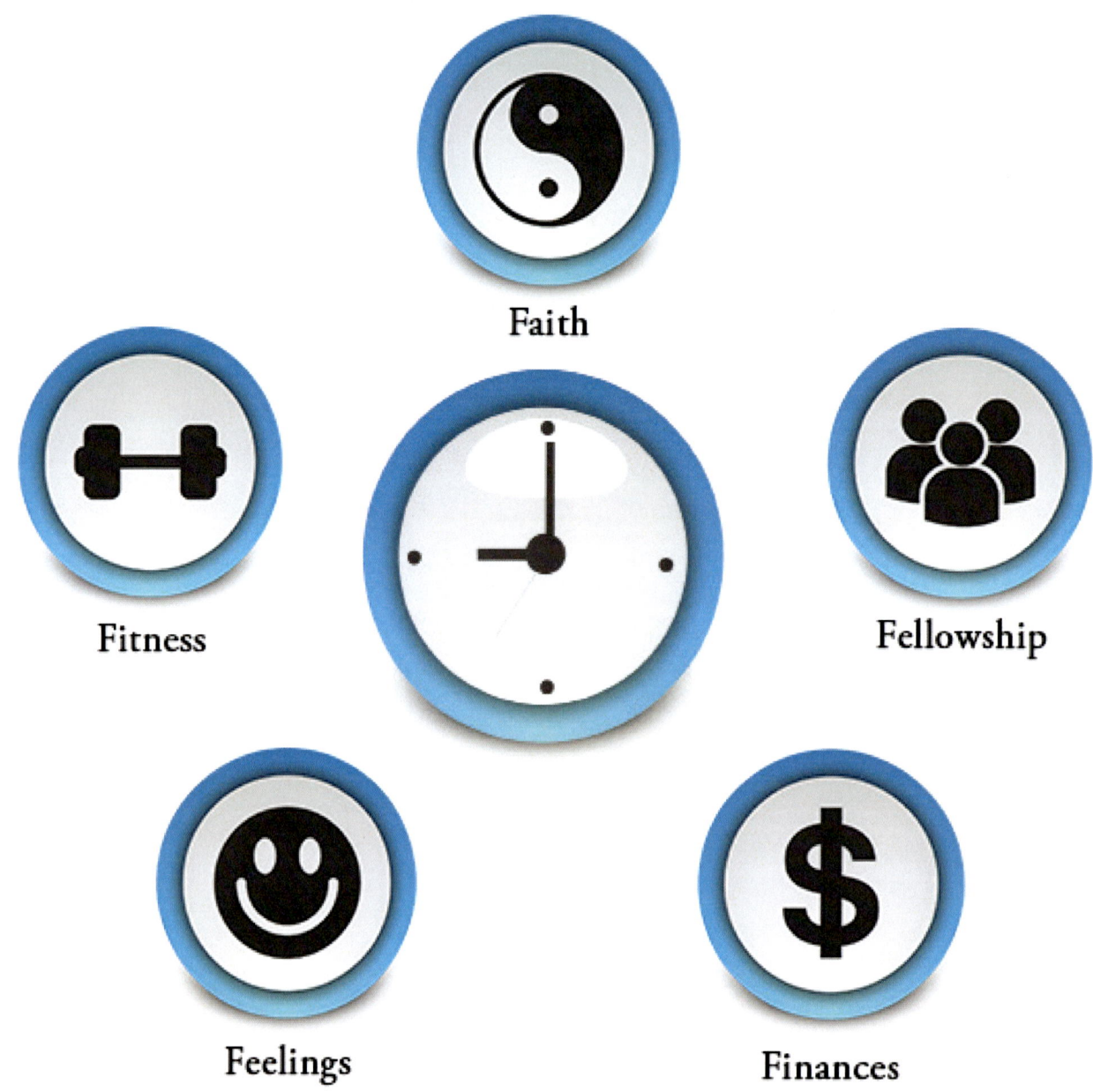

THE 5 KINGDOMS OF LIFE

THE **5** KINGDOMS | WORLDS OF LIFE

The 24 Hour Blueprint program deals with life beyond the traditional techniques and strategies of time management. It addresses something common to all human beings and it's this: meaning. Human beings are meaning creating creatures; we're storytellers. And when there isn't a story to tell, life loses its *meaning* or allure. In this program, we teach that there are 5 primary areas we want to not only tell stories in, but to share and engage with. And they are known as the 5 Kingdoms.

"The 5 Kingdoms" is perhaps the most significant concept of this program. The original sense and meaning of the word kingdom refers to one of the realms of nature as well as kingship, dominion, and rule. The idea behind this concept within this program is to trigger a thought pattern and life view that most of us seldom consider in our general, everyday life. This is the life view of "I am royalty an I am sovereign over how my life goes."

Few of us feel like royalty on a daily basis and as a result expect very little of ourselves and others. Taking this a step further, few of us exert the inner power required to manage areas of our lives with the same sense of authority that a royal figure would exercise. To see a shift in our use of time requires this kind of paradigm adjustment. This section gives you the opportunity to begin to experience the power you truly have over your life and the activities that matter to you most.

So, each kingdom is essentially an area of life that includes sub-areas and activities that you are already engaged in. This will all make a lot of sense as you take on this exercise.

There are 5 Kingdoms or areas of life. And they are:

1. Faith (Spirituality)

2. Fellowship (Relationships)

3. Finances (Money)

4. Feelings (Emotional States)

5. Fitness (Physical Body, our Possessions & Environment)

Every kingdom of life has primary activities required to keep it vibrant and working. Let's take **Fitness** at the body level for example. To stay alive and healthy, it'd be optimal to eat, drink, sleep, exercise, and take care of your mind through spiritual and social activities. That seems simple enough. However, there are daily, weekly and monthly tasks that you must fulfill in order to honor this kingdom. Some of these tasks may include keeping a grocery shopping list of foods you must have to stay energized or logging how many hours of rest you're getting.

In addition, you may need to drive to the store on a particular night of the week vs. daily to save time energy and money. Of course, once your meals and shakes are prepared, you'll need time at the gym to put that food to work for you. To keep muscles recovering well, your sleep patterns will have to follow suit. These are just some things to consider when addressing this kingdom of life.

This all sounds nice until it's time to live it; and that's what this section is about. We all know a lot of how-to's, but when it comes to doing, and doing those things on time, effectively and efficiently – that's another conversation. This section will help by giving you an honest baseline to take actions from.

Let's start with using the table below. On a scale of 1 – 5, with 5 being excellent and 1 being poor, score your performance on the tasks noted below.

Kingdom of Fitness: (Example)

List 3 to 5 Primary Activities. Rate yourself on a Scale of [1 to 5]:

	Actions | Activities	Circle One:
1.	Shop for Fresh Groceries on Sundays	[1 - (2) - 3 - 4 - 5]
2.	iAttend Yoga class on Thursday	[(1) - 2 - 3 - 4 - 5]
3.	iRead fitness magazine or book(s)	[(1) - 2 - 3 - 4 - 5]
4.	iSleep 6 hours to 8 hours daily	[1 - (2) - 3 - 4 - 5]
5.	iDrink 4 – 6 glasses of water a day	[(1) - 2 - 3 - 4 - 5]

Add numbers above to get **Total Rating**: ___7___

Divide Total Rating [7] by number of Activities [5] **Kingdom Score**: ___1.4___

Emoticon Legend:
Your Score can be interpreted using the emoticon legend to the right. Pick the number closest to your Kingdom Score legend to the right.

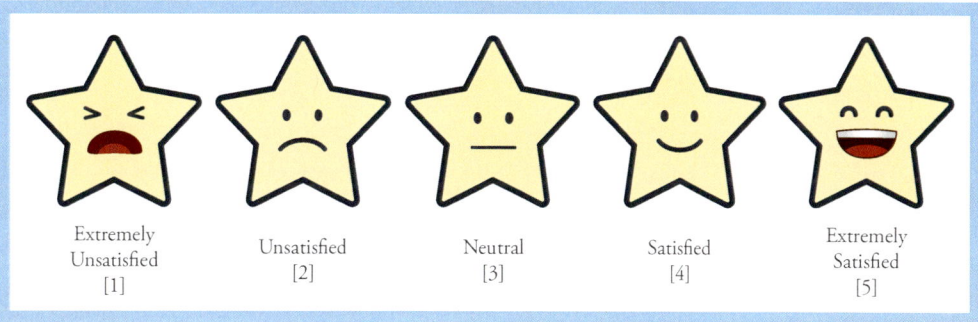

| Extremely Unsatisfied [1] | Unsatisfied [2] | Neutral [3] | Satisfied [4] | Extremely Satisfied [5] |

If you received a Kingdom Score of 1.4, it reflects that you are between Extreme Unsatisfaction and Unsatisfaction in the area of Fitness or any area that you assess and get a similar score.

That's not good, but the good news is that you now know and can change it

CALCULATIONS – HOW TO CRUNCH THE NUMBERS

Total Rating – To calculate total rating, add all numbers you've circled for each activity and write the total in the space provided. The highest total rating you can get is 5 for each activity, which means you can have 25 points maximum if you rated 5 for each task.

Kingdom Score – To calculate your kingdom score, divide your Total Rating by the number of primary activities or actions listed.

i.e. If you have 5 tasks in a kingdom to perform, then you would divide your total by "5" because that's the number of tasks you have in that kingdom. If you had 6 tasks, then you'd divide by 6. You get the idea.

What does this mean? With a score of 1.4, it's evident that my Fitness Kingdom is poorly tended to. I have a choice to make and actions to take to address what would be required to get it from 1.4 to, let's say, a 4. At this point I now have a meaningful place to come from in scheduling myself rather than judging myself for what I'm not doing. That's the power of this exercise.

Final Instructions

This can be done for all kingdoms of life and even sub kingdoms. If perhaps you were part of the choir or a committee as your spiritual place of worship, this area would be a sub-kingdom and there'd be activities you could note and rate yourself in. The exercise can be endless, but keep to the basic areas at first. You can develop mastery later.

If you're ready, I invite you to perform this exercise on other areas of life that matter to you. A blank assessment document has been provided for you to utilize for this purpose.

Watch how it's done (Click the Video Button Below)
www.video.24hourblueprint.com

Trouble seeing the video? Click here

5 KINGDOMS ASSESSMENT

Kingdom of (Circle One):   (Other) _____

*List 3 to 5 **Primary Activities**.* *Rate yourself on a Scale of* [1
to 5]:

Actions | Activities	Circle One:
1. _____	[1 - 2 - 3 - 4 - 5]
2. _____	[1 - 2 - 3 - 4 - 5]
3. _____	[1 - 2 - 3 - 4 - 5]
4. _____	[1 - 2 - 3 - 4 - 5]
5. _____	[1 - 2 - 3 - 4 - 5]

Total Rating: _____

Kingdom Score: _____

Kingdom of (Circle One):   (Other) _____

*List 3 to 5 **Primary Activities**.* *Rate yourself on a Scale of* [1
to 5]:

Actions | Activities	Circle One:
1. _____	[1 - 2 - 3 - 4 - 5]
2. _____	[1 - 2 - 3 - 4 - 5]
3. _____	[1 - 2 - 3 - 4 - 5]
4. _____	[1 - 2 - 3 - 4 - 5]
5. _____	[1 - 2 - 3 - 4 - 5]

Total Rating: _____

Kingdom Score: _____

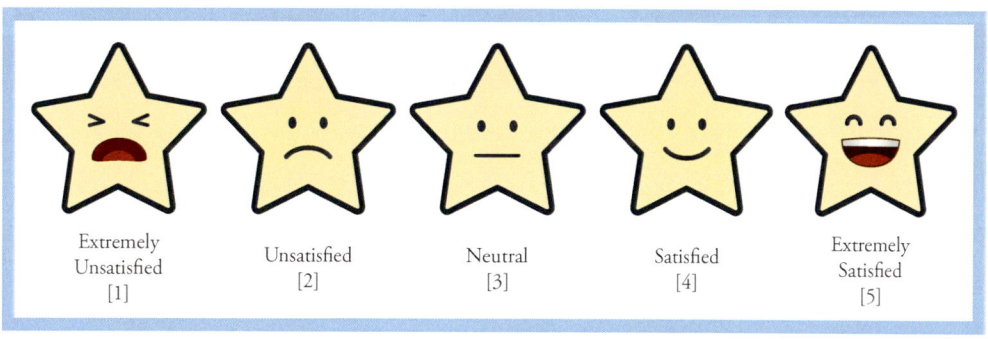

| Extremely Unsatisfied [1] | Unsatisfied [2] | Neutral [3] | Satisfied [4] | Extremely Satisfied [5] |

TIME MANAGEMENT TOOLS

After doing your kingdom assessment, it's time to get to work. To do the job right, you'll need the right tools. You've heard that before - right? Well, that still holds true here. And here's what we need to get clear about. What tools are you currently using to assist you with leveraging your time? Notice I didn't say manage? I might even slip and use the term "manage" when describing what can be done with time, but that's not true. Time can be honored for what it is or leveraged. That's about it. Everything else that you hear about time will more than likely be great advertising. With that being said, we need to take inventory of what you're currently using and make sure that you're making the most of it. Which of the following tools are you currently using to honor or leverage your time?

- Microsoft Outlook
- Google Calendar
- Franklin-Covey Planner
- At-A-Glance
- Phone Calendar
- Other
- Or nothing aka "I don't need to write it down, I can remember everything"

Now, write down the tool you use below in the spaces provided.

I use _____ <<<(Insert tool name) because….

(Write your top 3 reasons for using this particular tool)

1. _____
   _____

2. _____
   _____

3. _____
   _____

Last but not least, if there was one thing you could change about this tool, what would it be? And why?

The one thing I would change about this tool is:

_____

And that's because…

_____

PREPARATION CHECKLIST

To go on this journey, I recommend tools that will make it a little bit easier and even more fun to experience. Below are some digital and non-digital tools that can be used to bring peace of mind to you.

Non-Digital

- ☐ Small Compact Notebook (Capture Tool)
- ☐ Recording Device
- ☐ Time-Graphic Display (Daytimer, Daily Planner, Calendar)
- ☐ 3-ring binder (or spiral bound)
- ☐ Dividers (if using binders)

Digital

- ☐ Cell Phone
- ☐ Microsoft Outlook
- ☐ Google Account (for Google Calendar)
- ☐ Other online calendar system

Reference Material

- ☐ Book, **HEROmanity: 24 Hours to a HEROic Life**
- ☐ Subscription to HEROmanity online or offline training (incl. 24 Hour Blueprint training)
- ☐ 3-Week Look-Ahead Template (featuring time usage calculator)
- ☐ Daily Intentions & Outcomes template
- ☐ Task-Event list (Digital Worksheet)
- ☐ Time Usage Display Chart
- ☐ Calendar (1 Month Display)
- ☐ Agenda template
- ☐ Executive Contacts Template
- ☐ Monthly Budget Template
- ☐ Grocery Template
- ☐ Recommended reading list (at the end of this playbook)
- ☐ Glossary of Terms

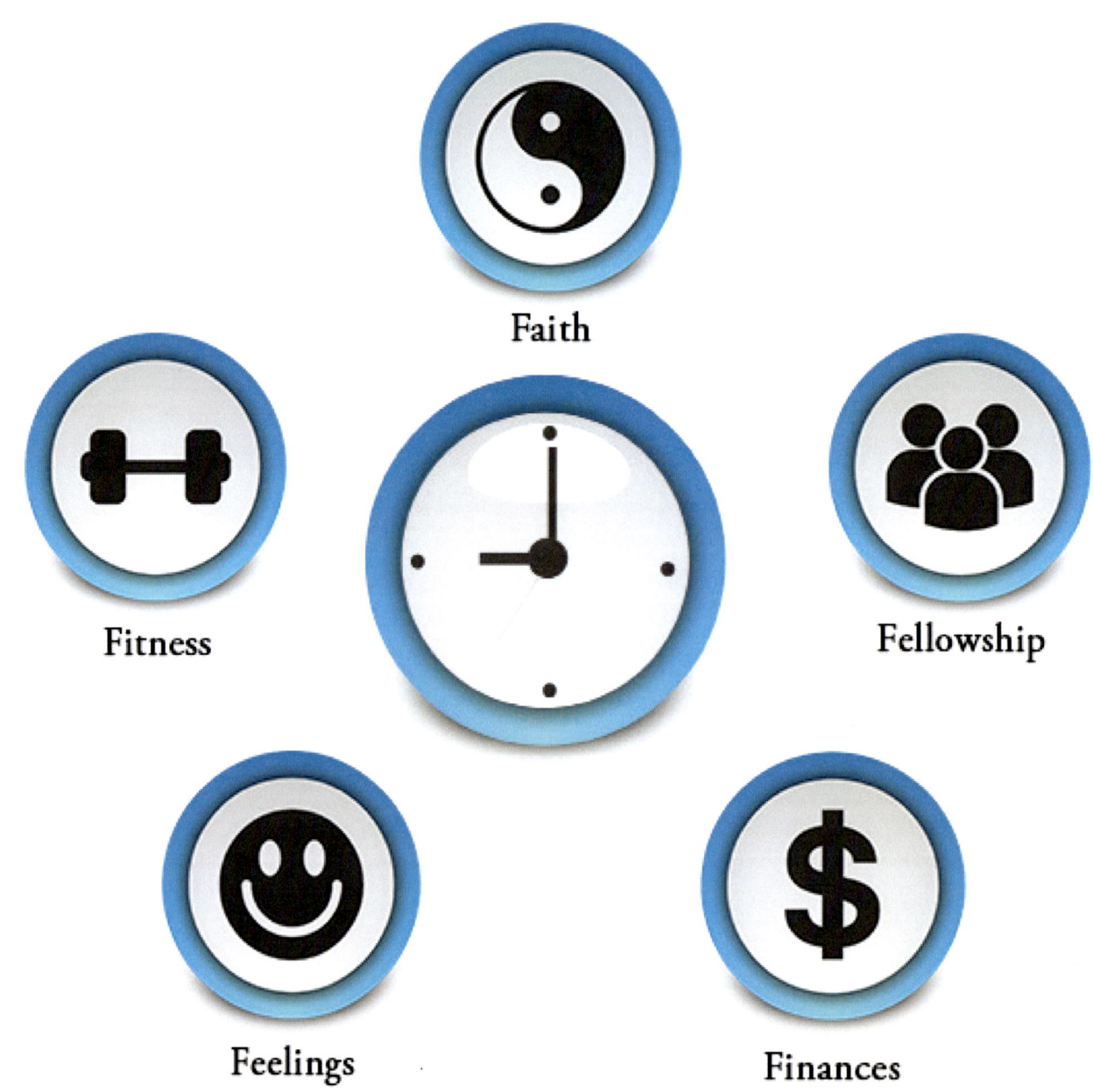

Faith

Fitness

Fellowship

Feelings

Finances

THE 5 KINGDOMS DAILY PERFORMANCE TRACKING

KINGDOM DAILY PERFORMANCE TRACKING

If you were a professional and or business person reading this playbook, one of the kingdoms that might matter to you most could be the Financial Kingdom, and your career or business would be a sub-kingdom you can focus on. As a result, your career and business' performance is the primary thing you will likely want to use this program to take to the next level.

So, you can ask yourself questions like how am I doing in my career or business? Am I on track to get the bonus, secure a new position or hit the next business milestone? These are questions your supervisors or managers might get and you perhaps are asking. But the answer is easy to address if you've tracked the little things along the way. Here's a sample of questions that you might want to answer for yourself before running into the manager's office for assurance.

- **Training and Development:** Have I been reading and taking the needed trainings to move forward powerfully?
- **Projects:** Have I been completing ALL projects as expected or better?
- **Leadership:** Have I empowered others to perform or criticized them?
- **Engagement:** Have I been enthusiastically engaged in my work or business?
- **Promptness:** Have I been showing up and completing projects early if not, on time at the latest?
- **Preparation:** Preparing for every meeting, event thoroughly?
- **Follow-Up:** Have I made it a practice to review notes after meetings to make sure no actions fall through the cracks?

It may seem tedious to ask these questions over and over again, but so is it to shoot 100's or 1000's of freethrows before a game and sometimes after. This program is about a championship mindset and as such there are tools to facilitate or cultivate it. The sample table below is something you can use to go over your day to trigger assuring thoughts. I've used the example above to show how something like this can come in handy. "✓" means the task was done and "Ø" means nothing was done. A "-" means the task wasn't scheduled for that specific day.

Kingdom Tasks	Sun	Mon	Tues	Wed	Thu	Fri	Sat	Comments
Dates:								
Career | Business								
iReadTradeLiterature/Blogs	✓	-	-	-	-	-	-	
iDocumentAndTrackResultsWeekly	∅	∅	✓	✓	✓	✓	✓	
iSpeakUpInMeetings	-	∅	✓	-	✓	-	-	
iArrive10minsEarlyToMeetings	-	✓	✓	∅	∅	-	-	
iTakeAdvantageOfOpenDoorPolicy	-	∅	✓	∅	✓	∅	-	
iScheduleContinuingEducationEvents	✓	-	-	-	-	-	-	
Score:	67%	25%	100%	33%	75%	50%	100%	

The table above is again, a sample of a digital worksheet available through the 24 Hour Blueprint program which you can use to create your own tasks and trigger your thoughts to stay in the game of greater life performance. As simple as it looks, you'd be surprised how clear and competitive you become when it comes to making sure that you can score 100% by completing the tasks for an area of life that's important to you such as scheduling continuing education events on a Sunday!

Kingdom Tasks	Sun	Mon	Tues	Wed	Thu	Fri	Sat	Comments
Dates:								
Faith (%) Spirituality > Spirit[U]al Empowerment								
Score:								

Fellowship (@) Social > [Soul]cial Connections & Support								
Score:								

Finance ($) Money > Financial Em[POWER]ment								
Score:								

Feelings :) Emotions > Energy or Inner[Chi]-In-Motion								
Score:								

Fitness :[#]: Physical > Kingdom Man[AGE]ment								
Score:								

The best news I have to share about the exercise above is that it never gets old and once it becomes a habit, you'll never be able to remember a time when you were NOT doing it. A blank version of the above table is provided below for your reference.

Note: You may copy the Kingdom Tracking Worksheet to assist you in tracking your habitual performance as a professional or entrepreneur – based on your current your role.

Watch how it's done (Click the Video Button Below)
www.video.24hourblueprint.com

Trouble seeing the video? Click here

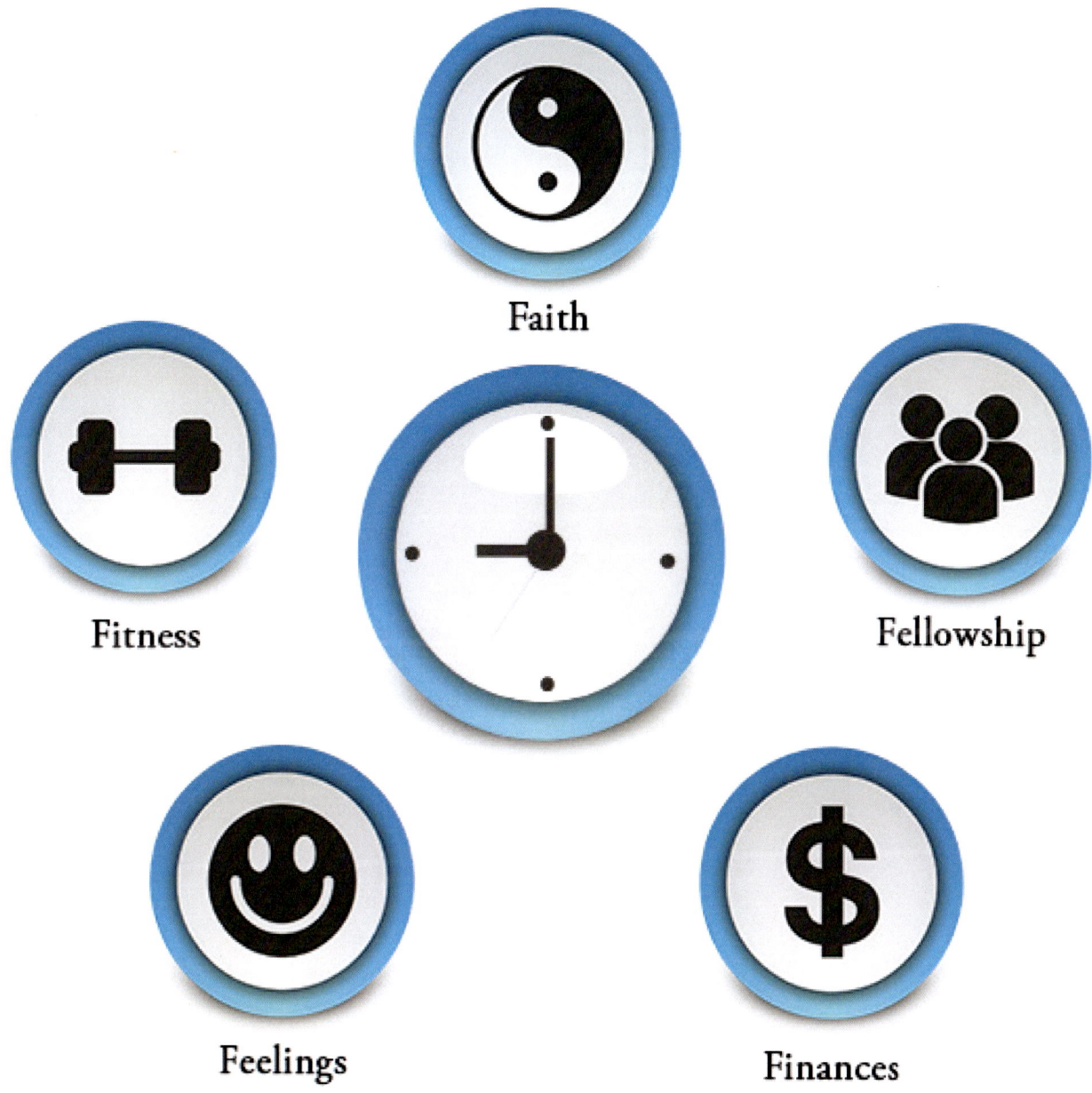

Faith

Fitness

Fellowship

Feelings

Finances

THE 3-WEEK LOOK-AHEAD METHOD

THE **3**-WEEK LOOK-AHEAD METHOD

It is a mistake to look too far ahead. Only one link in the chain of destiny can be handled at a time.
—Sir Winston Churchill

Planning vs. Looking Ahead

This section is where the rubber of this playbook meets the road. Regardless of the many concepts we've introduced in this playbook, you must put them into action in your life in order to manage it.

So, let's start with defining some terms.

planning

> *noun*
> 1. the act or process of making or carrying out plans; specifically the establishment of goals, policies, and procedures for a social or economic unit.
>
> > "city planning" "business planning"
> > synonyms: preparation(s), organization, arrangement, design.

look

> *verb*
> 1. direct one's gaze toward someone or something or in a specified direction.
>
> > "people were looking at him"
> > synonyms: glance at, gaze at, stare at, gape at, peer at.
>
> 2. have the appearance or give the impression of being.
>
> > "her father looked unhappy"
> > synonyms: seem, seem to be, appear, appear to be, have the appearance/air of being, give the impression of being, give every appearance/indication of being, strike someone as being
>
> *noun*
> 1. an act of directing one's gaze in order to see someone or something.
>
> > "let me get a closer look"
> > synonyms: glance, view, examination, study, inspection, observation, scan, survey, peep, peek, glimpse, gaze, stare.

With these terms defined, we can now move into using the next tool, the **3-Week Look-Ahead**. Although we've come a long way with respect to time management systems, some of them still remain stiff and counter-intuitive. Consider which planner gives you a better sense of what's happening in a 7 day period of time.

EXAMPLE PLANNERS

Example 1:
Standard Weekly Calendar/Planner

Example 2:
Timed Weekly Calendar/Planner

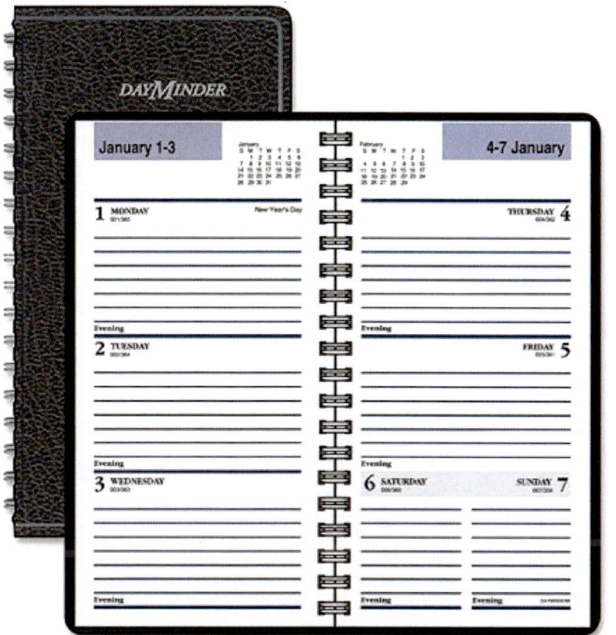

Note: This format is helpful but has a limit when your task load rises beyond the space provided.

Note: The calendar format here also can be found in your local office supply store today - Office Depot, STAPLES, even Target. But the pitfall of this model is that the standard 8:00am-5:00pm time-frame they sometimes have doesn't work for most people anymore. Our lives today are way more complicated, hectic, and demanding since our lives don't stop at 5pm. And the planners that use this model don't reflect that we're 24-7 operators now.

These planning systems all fall short in allowing you to see the ebb and flow of daily life. You would have to thumb through page after page of days and weeks in order to see the rhythms that impact you, the rhythms that either work for you, or work against you. Given how short a month is, the ability to see 3 weeks ahead has a major impact on the psyche and planning future workloads.

THE 24 HOUR BLUEPRINT DIFFERENCE

Example 3:
The 24 Hour Blueprint Model

> **Note:** This model of displaying a week is uncommon. However, if blocks of activities have been set aside the week becomes dramatically more manageable. This is because of the user being able to see it in one portrait and landscape view.

In example 3, each week has its own page! As simple as this subtle change is, it's remarkable that you cannot go to any office supply store and easily find a display like the two page arrangement above, with each week having its on page and the time extending to midnight. I've seen the previous two versions for the past 10+ years and nothing has changed until I created my own planning sheets out of frustration.

The spatial-intuitive way to view time matches more the model above than the previous two. The advantage is the absolute decrease in the anxiety the user has from not knowing what's really coming down the pipe and not having to work too hard to keep activities in their minds straight.

To fill the week with the appropriate activities, you can use a calendar like the one shown below. Microsoft has an excel template and Outlook has a calendar like it which you can print and use. On the next few pages, you'll find a workable example of the ease and flow of using a calendar as described.

Watch the video below to see how this works or you can start using the template and get to work immediately entering your activities. The digital worksheet version is a great place to start.

For more on this, watch the video by pressing play.
OR visit www.video.24hourblueprint.com

Note: The best news I have to share about this exercise is that it never gets old and once it becomes a habit, you'll never be able to remember a time when you were NOT doing it. A blank version of the above table is provided below for your reference.

3-Week Look-Ahead

	SUNDAY	MONDAY	TUESDAY	WEDNESDAY	THURSDAY	FRIDAY	SATURDAY
12:00 AM							
12:30 AM							
1:00 AM							
1:30 AM							
2:00 AM							
2:30 AM							
3:00 AM							
3:30 AM							
4:00 AM							
4:30 AM							
5:00 AM							
5:30 AM							
6:00 AM							
6:30 AM							
7:00 AM							
7:30 AM							
8:00 AM							
8:30 AM							
9:00 AM							
9:30 AM							
10:00 AM							
10:30 AM							
11:00 AM							
11:30 AM							
12:00 PM							
12:30 PM							
1:00 PM							
1:30 PM							
2:00 PM							
2:30 PM							
3:00 PM							
3:30 PM							
4:00 PM							
4:30 PM							
5:00 PM							
5:30 PM							
6:00 PM							
6:30 PM							
7:00 PM							
7:30 PM							
8:00 PM							
8:30 PM							
9:00 PM							
9:30 PM							
10:00 PM							
10:30 PM							
11:00 PM							
11:30 PM							

DAILY INTENTIONS & OUTCOMES

Sunday

☺	
👥	
$	
☯	
🏋	

Monday

☺	
👥	
$	
☯	
🏋	

Tuesday

☺	
👥	
$	
☯	
🏋	

Wednesday

☺	
👥	
$	
☯	
🏋	

Thursday

☺	
👥	
$	
☯	
🏋	

Friday

☺	
👥	
$	
☯	
🏋	

Saturday

☺	
👥	
$	
☯	
🏋	

Notes

☺	
👥	
$	
☯	
🏋	

DAILY INTENTIONS & OUTCOMES

Sunday

Thursday

Monday

Friday

Tuesday

Saturday

Wednesday

Notes

3-Week Look-Ahead

	SUNDAY	MONDAY	TUESDAY	WEDNESDAY	THURSDAY	FRIDAY	SATURDAY
12:00 AM							
12:30 AM							
1:00 AM							
1:30 AM							
2:00 AM							
2:30 AM							
3:00 AM							
3:30 AM							
4:00 AM							
4:30 AM							
5:00 AM							
5:30 AM							
6:00 AM							
6:30 AM							
7:00 AM							
7:30 AM							
8:00 AM							
8:30 AM							
9:00 AM							
9:30 AM							
10:00 AM							
10:30 AM							
11:00 AM							
11:30 AM							
12:00 PM							
12:30 PM							
1:00 PM							
1:30 PM							
2:00 PM							
2:30 PM							
3:00 PM							
3:30 PM							
4:00 PM							
4:30 PM							
5:00 PM							
5:30 PM							
6:00 PM							
6:30 PM							
7:00 PM							
7:30 PM							
8:00 PM							
8:30 PM							
9:00 PM							
9:30 PM							
10:00 PM							
10:30 PM							
11:00 PM							
11:30 PM							

3-Week Look-Ahead

	Sunday	Monday	Tuesday	Wednesday	Thursday	Friday	Saturday
12:00 AM							
12:30 AM							
1:00 AM							
1:30 AM							
2:00 AM							
2:30 AM							
3:00 AM							
3:30 AM							
4:00 AM							
4:30 AM							
5:00 AM							
5:30 AM							
6:00 AM							
6:30 AM							
7:00 AM							
7:30 AM							
8:00 AM							
8:30 AM							
9:00 AM							
9:30 AM							
10:00 AM							
10:30 AM							
11:00 AM							
11:30 AM							
12:00 PM							
12:30 PM							
1:00 PM							
1:30 PM							
2:00 PM							
2:30 PM							
3:00 PM							
3:30 PM							
4:00 PM							
4:30 PM							
5:00 PM							
5:30 PM							
6:00 PM							
6:30 PM							
7:00 PM							
7:30 PM							
8:00 PM							
8:30 PM							
9:00 PM							
9:30 PM							
10:00 PM							
10:30 PM							
11:00 PM							
11:30 PM							

DAILY INTENTIONS & OUTCOMES

Sunday

😊	
👥	
$	
☯	
🏋	

Thursday

😊	
👥	
$	
☯	
🏋	

Monday

😊	
👥	
$	
☯	
🏋	

Friday

😊	
👥	
$	
☯	
🏋	

Tuesday

😊	
👥	
$	
☯	
🏋	

Saturday

😊	
👥	
$	
☯	
🏋	

Wednesday

😊	
👥	
$	
☯	
🏋	

Notes

😊	
👥	
$	
☯	
🏋	

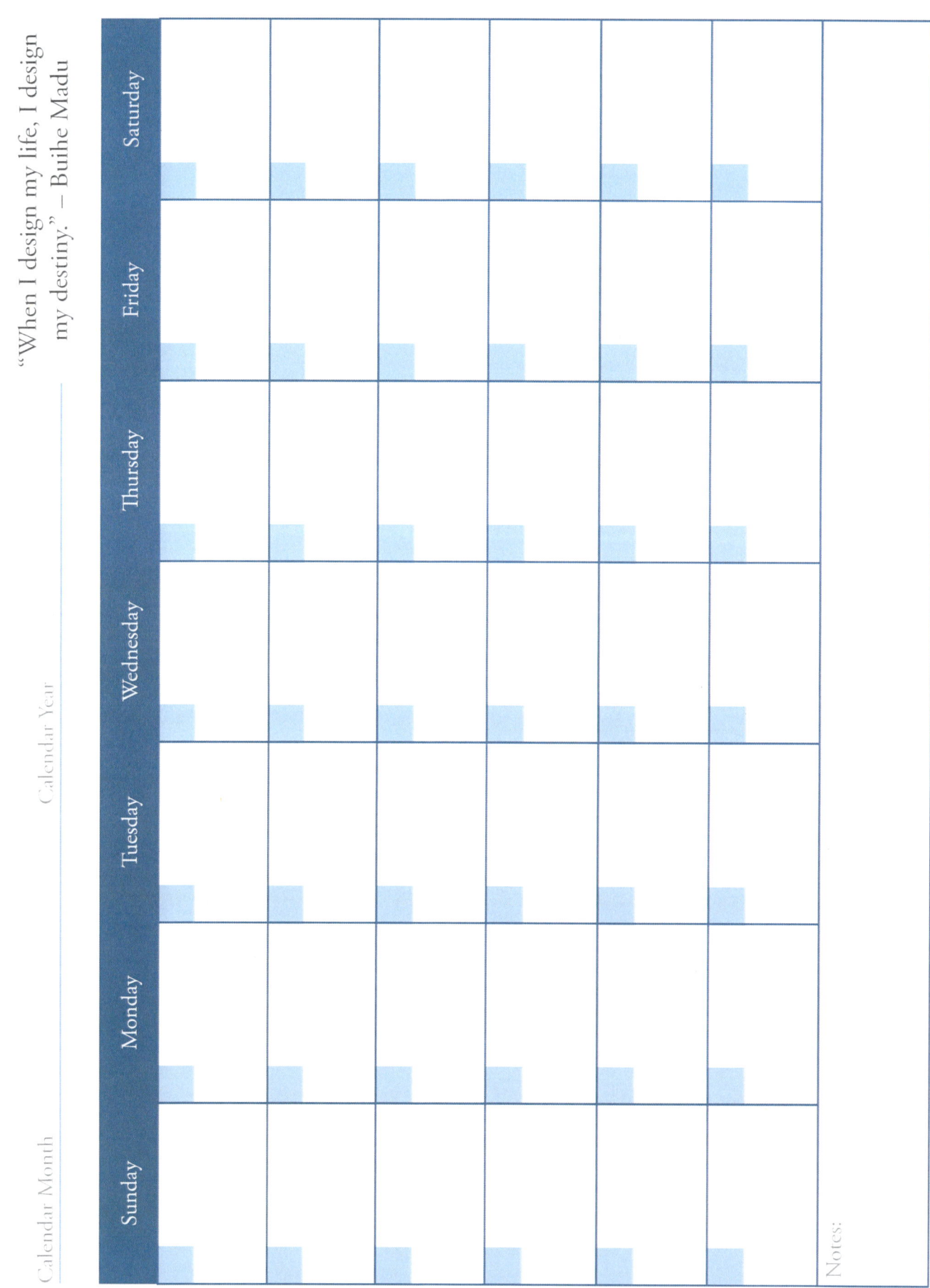

Calendar Month _____   Calendar Year _____

"When I design my life, I design my destiny." – Buihe Madu

Sunday	Monday	Tuesday	Wednesday	Thursday	Friday	Saturday

Notes:

WHAT'S NEXT? FINAL INSTRUCTIONS

This is it. You're done for now. Yes, there is so much more to learn, but these are the basics that you can build mastery from. So here are some final instructions I have for you.

1. ☑ **Become a 24 Hour Blueprint Tribe Member** TODAY so that you can get first access to exclusive content, trainings, offers and more! Start here:

2. ☑ **Access to downloadable** sheets of this playbook at: www.download.24hourblueprint.com

3. ☑ **Start filling the calendar or 3-Week Look-Ahead sheets** with all your life activities i.e. spiritual, social, financial activities and times, etc. Don't forget to schedule special activities like holiday breaks or anniversaries as well.

4. Commit to mastery by discovering the 24 hour blueprint coaching program here.

ARE YOU READY TO BE COACHED TOWARD MASTERY?

Yes, I Am Coachable!

Or visit
www.coaching.24hourblueprint.com

BONUS SHEETS
(TEST DRIVE THE SYSTEM)

NOTE:

THIS SECTION GIVES YOU A SENSE OF WHAT YOUR PERFECT DAY, WEEK OR MONTH(S) AHEAD COULD LOOK LIKE USING THE 24 HOUR BLUEPRINT SYSTEM. IT INCLUDES THE FOLLOWING:

✔ 3-Month set of the Wall of Intentions sheets (This goes on your office wall or similar workspace surface)

✔ A set of 3-Week Look-Ahead (3 sheets total)

✔ A set of Daily Intentions and Outcomes sheets (These are the sheets you see in between the 3-Week Look-Ahead sheets)

✔ 5 Brain Dump sheets (Use one for Each Kingdom)

✔ 5 Agenda Execution Sheets (One for each of the Brain Dump sheets)

✔ A 5 Week 1-Page Accountability sheet

✔ 7-Day Daily Task Planner sheets

WALL OF INTENTIONS
CALENDAR SHEETS

About Wall of Intentions Calendar Sheets

Sometimes we're so close to our goals it's hard to step back and see the big picture as well as the actions we need to take over the days, weeks and months ahead in order to achieve them.

The Wall of Intentions sheet allows you to map your goals out as far as you can imagine months at a time and literally take a step back. As you take a step back, you're able to see the smaller actions you'll need to take. And as you do that, you'll notice which weeks of each month those smaller actions should be taken to get you across the finish line.

How to use it:

1. Tape the Wall of Intentions sheet on a wall

2. Write the month(s) each sheet represents in the center of each sheet

3. Grab a stack of sticky notes

4. Write your goals on the sticky notes

5. Place the goals on the month(s) you expect to reach the goal(s) noted.

6. Sit still for 5-15 mins (You can set an alarm to time yourself)

7. Identify and use additional sticky notes to write down the small steps you'll need to take between now and the goal deadlines based on your sticky notes

8. Place these sticky notes in the weeks the small steps need to be taken

Wall of Intentions

WEEK 1

WEEK 2

WEEK 3

WEEK 4

Wall of Intentions

WEEK 1

WEEK 2

WEEK 3

WEEK 4

Wall of Intentions

WEEK 1

WEEK 2

WEEK 3

WEEK 4

3-WEEK LOOK-AHEAD WITH INTENTIONS AND OUTCOMES SHEETS

About 3-Week Look-Ahead With Intentions and Outcomes Sheets

Daily life can get so overwhelming, it becomes difficult to come up for air and find the time to prepare or plan for tomorrow's activities let alone plan for tasks a week or two ahead.

Unfortunately, the result of not being able to think far enough ahead is sometimes a slow response to changes in plans and a backlog of regrets and "I wish I would've taken care of this last week" thoughts.

The 3-Week Look-Ahead sheets make it easy at a glance to see what's coming up - not just one week in advance, not two, but three! Being able to see this far in advance at a glance brings the calmness and the peace of mind you'll need to stay focused on your big picture goals and not get caught off guard by daily dramas.

The Intentions and Outcomes sheets in between the 3-Week Look-Ahead sheets are ideal for writing the daily tasks that you'll have time for within the times you've blocked off using your 3-Week Look-Ahead sheets.

How to use it:

1. Set 30 minutes aside for planning your week (Remember to set your timer when doing this exercise)

2. On your 3-Week Look-Ahead sheet, block out the most time consuming events of your week i.e. commuting, sleep, work, self care etc.

3. Do this two more times for the next week and the week after

4. Notice how much time remains in the gaps between time blocks

5. Make a note of what you'll do in those gaps on your Weekly Intentions and Outcomes sheets

WEEKLY INTENTIONS & OUTCOMES

AM	PM
Si Nun Cum Non	

	AM	PM
Sunday		
Monday		
Tuesday		
Wednesday		
Thursday		
Friday		
Saturday		
NOTES & ACCOUNTABILITY		[ ] iComplete Weekly Review of My Actions. My Score is: _____ [ ] iSchedule Actions to Improve My Score [ ] iUpdate next week's Intentions and Actions [ ] iMake Adjustments on the 3-Week Look-Ahead Sheet [ ] iSchedule a Coaching Call to improve Results [ ] iShare My Wins with the Community and/or Accountability Partner

3-Week Look-Ahead

	Dec 31 Sunday	Jan 1 Monday	Jan 2 Tuesday	Jan 3 Wednesday	Jan 4 Thursday	Jan 5 Friday	Jan 6 Saturday
12:00 AM							
12:30 AM							
1:00 AM							
1:30 AM							
2:00 AM							
2:30 AM							
3:00 AM							
3:30 AM							
4:00 AM							
4:30 AM							
5:00 AM							
5:30 AM							
6:00 AM							
6:30 AM							
7:00 AM							
7:30 AM							
8:00 AM							
8:30 AM							
9:00 AM							
9:30 AM							
10:00 AM							
10:30 AM							
11:00 AM							
11:30 AM							
12:00 PM							
12:30 PM							
1:00 PM							
1:30 PM							
2:00 PM							
2:30 PM							
3:00 PM							
3:30 PM							
4:00 PM							
4:30 PM							
5:00 PM							
5:30 PM							
6:00 PM							
6:30 PM							
7:00 PM							
7:30 PM							
8:00 PM							
8:30 PM							
9:00 PM							
9:30 PM							
10:00 PM							
10:30 PM							
11:00 PM							
11:30 PM							

3-Week Look-Ahead

	Jan 7 Sunday	Jan 8 Monday	Jan 9 Tuesday	Jan 10 Wednesday	Jan 11 Thursday	Jan 12 Friday	Jan 13 Saturday
12:00 AM							
12:30 AM							
1:00 AM							
1:30 AM							
2:00 AM							
2:30 AM							
3:00 AM							
3:30 AM							
4:00 AM							
4:30 AM							
5:00 AM							
5:30 AM							
6:00 AM							
6:30 AM							
7:00 AM							
7:30 AM							
8:00 AM							
8:30 AM							
9:00 AM							
9:30 AM							
10:00 AM							
10:30 AM							
11:00 AM							
11:30 AM							
12:00 PM							
12:30 PM							
1:00 PM							
1:30 PM							
2:00 PM							
2:30 PM							
3:00 PM							
3:30 PM							
4:00 PM							
4:30 PM							
5:00 PM							
5:30 PM							
6:00 PM							
6:30 PM							
7:00 PM							
7:30 PM							
8:00 PM							
8:30 PM							
9:00 PM							
9:30 PM							
10:00 PM							
10:30 PM							
11:00 PM							
11:30 PM							

WEEKLY INTENTIONS & OUTCOMES

	AM	PM
	Si Nun Cum Non	
Sunday		
Monday		
Tuesday		
Wednesday		
Thursday		
Friday		
Saturday		

NOTES & ACCOUNTABILITY

[ ] iComplete Weekly Review of My Actions. My Score is: ___.___
[ ] iSchedule Actions to Improve My Score
[ ] iUpdate next week's Intentions and Actions
[ ] iMake Adjustments on the 3-Week Look-Ahead Sheet
[ ] iSchedule a Coaching Call to improve Results
[ ] iShare My Wins with the Community and/or Accountability Partner

Weekly Intentions & Outcomes

	AM	PM
	Si Nun Cum Non	
Sunday		
Monday		
Tuesday		
Wednesday		
Thursday		
Friday		
Saturday		
NOTES & ACCOUNTABILITY		[ ] iComplete Weekly Review of My Actions. My Score is: _____
		[ ] iSchedule Actions to Improve My Score
		[ ] iUpdate next week's Intentions and Actions
		[ ] iMake Adjustments on the 3-Week Look-Ahead Sheet
		[ ] iSchedule a Coaching Call to improve Results
		[ ] iShare My Wins with the Community and/or Accountability Partner

3-Week Look-Ahead

	Jan 14 Sunday	Jan 15 Monday	Jan 16 Tuesday	Jan 17 Wednesday	Jan 18 Thursday	Jan 19 Friday	Jan 20 Saturday
12:00 AM							
12:30 AM							
1:00 AM							
1:30 AM							
2:00 AM							
2:30 AM							
3:00 AM							
3:30 AM							
4:00 AM							
4:30 AM							
5:00 AM							
5:30 AM							
6:00 AM							
6:30 AM							
7:00 AM							
7:30 AM							
8:00 AM							
8:30 AM							
9:00 AM							
9:30 AM							
10:00 AM							
10:30 AM							
11:00 AM							
11:30 AM							
12:00 PM							
12:30 PM							
1:00 PM							
1:30 PM							
2:00 PM							
2:30 PM							
3:00 PM							
3:30 PM							
4:00 PM							
4:30 PM							
5:00 PM							
5:30 PM							
6:00 PM							
6:30 PM							
7:00 PM							
7:30 PM							
8:00 PM							
8:30 PM							
9:00 PM							
9:30 PM							
10:00 PM							
10:30 PM							
11:00 PM							
11:30 PM							

3-Week Look-Ahead

	Jan 21 Sunday	Jan 22 Monday	Jan 23 Tuesday	Jan 24 Wednesday	Jan 25 Thursday	Jan 26 Friday	Jan 27 Saturday
12:00 AM							
12:30 AM							
1:00 AM							
1:30 AM							
2:00 AM							
2:30 AM							
3:00 AM							
3:30 AM							
4:00 AM							
4:30 AM							
5:00 AM							
5:30 AM							
6:00 AM							
6:30 AM							
7:00 AM							
7:30 AM							
8:00 AM							
8:30 AM							
9:00 AM							
9:30 AM							
10:00 AM							
10:30 AM							
11:00 AM							
11:30 AM							
12:00 PM							
12:30 PM							
1:00 PM							
1:30 PM							
2:00 PM							
2:30 PM							
3:00 PM							
3:30 PM							
4:00 PM							
4:30 PM							
5:00 PM							
5:30 PM							
6:00 PM							
6:30 PM							
7:00 PM							
7:30 PM							
8:00 PM							
8:30 PM							
9:00 PM							
9:30 PM							
10:00 PM							
10:30 PM							
11:00 PM							
11:30 PM							

WEEKLY INTENTIONS & OUTCOMES

	AM	PM
	Si Nun Cum Non	
Sunday		
Monday		
Tuesday		
Wednesday		
Thursday		
Friday		
Saturday		
NOTES & ACCOUNTABILITY		[ ] iComplete Weekly Review of My Actions. My Score is: _____ [ ] iSchedule Actions to Improve My Score [ ] iUpdate next week's Intentions and Actions [ ] iMake Adjustments on the 3-Week Look-Ahead Sheet [ ] iSchedule a Coaching Call to improve Results [ ] iShare My Wins with the Community and/or Accountability Partner

BRAIN DUMP SHEETS

About the Brain Dump Sheets

With so much on our minds on any given day it's not a surprise that we walk into a kitchen and forget what we came in there for only to then walk away to return and still not remember.

The Brain Dump sheet gives us a place to remember and keep track of all the 100's of ideas and actions swimming in our heads with no place to pull up on shore by writing them down without self filtering or judgment.

And all it takes is setting aside as little as 5-15 minutes to jot down everything that's on our mind keeping us from thinking clearly or weighing our hearts down.

How to use it:

1. Set a timer for 5 mins

2. Write down everything that comes to mind in the area you are overwhelmed by. (Make sure you circle the kingdom at the top of the sheet if your thoughts are about a particular kingdom.)

3. Do not judge or be critical of what you write down. (Let it flow)

4. Stop when the alarm goes off

5. Note: If you need more time, repeat steps 1 - 4

6. On the Agenda sheet that follows take some of thoughts and ideas that you've written down and note them as actionable steps

7. These actions can be noted in your Weekly Intentions and Outcomes page(s) as needed when the time comes for you to take action on the tasks on this page

Brain Dump Exercise Sheets

 Faith  Fellowship  Finances  Feelings Fitness

Brain Dump Exercise Sheets

Faith

Fellowship

Finances

Feelings

Fitness

Do This Now: Note the Actions You Can Take Based on Your Brain Dump Below

☐ _____ ☐ _____

☐ _____ ☐ _____

☐ _____ ☐ _____

☐ _____ ☐ _____

☐ _____ ☐ _____

☐ _____ ☐ _____

☐ _____ ☐ _____

☐ _____ ☐ _____

☐ _____ ☐ _____

☐ _____ ☐ _____

☐ _____ ☐ _____

☐ _____ ☐ _____

Brain Dump Exercise Sheets

Faith   Fellowship   Finances   Feelings   Fitness

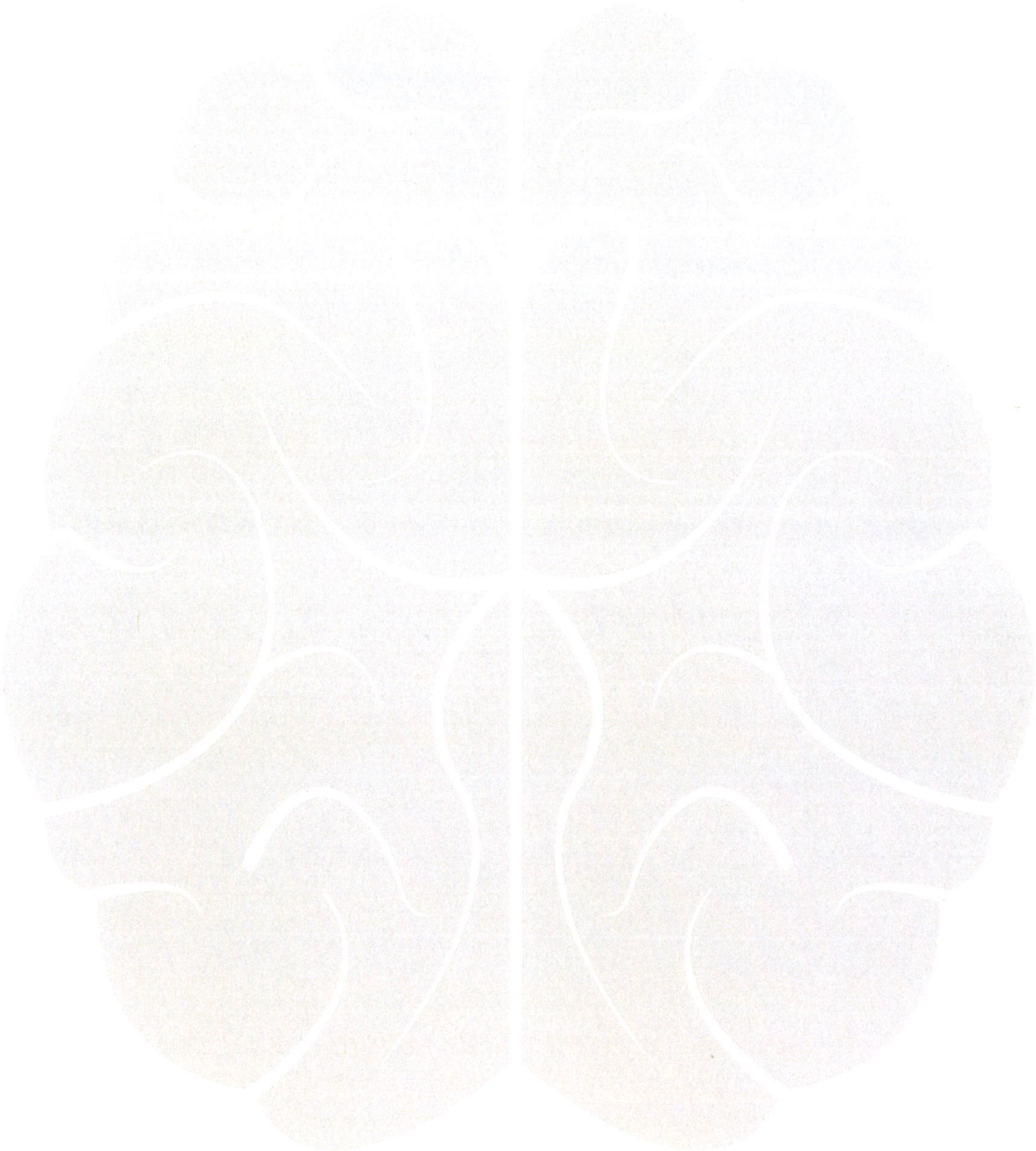

Brain Dump Exercise Sheets

Faith

Fellowship

Finances

Feelings

Fitness

Do This Now: Note the Actions You Can Take Based on Your Brain Dump Below

☐ _____   ☐ _____

☐ _____   ☐ _____

☐ _____   ☐ _____

☐ _____   ☐ _____

☐ _____   ☐ _____

☐ _____   ☐ _____

☐ _____   ☐ _____

☐ _____   ☐ _____

☐ _____   ☐ _____

☐ _____   ☐ _____

☐ _____   ☐ _____

☐ _____   ☐ _____

Brain Dump Exercise Sheets

Faith   Fellowship   Finances   Feelings   Fitness

Brain Dump Exercise Sheets

Faith   Fellowship   Finances   Feelings   Fitness

Do This Now: Note the Actions You Can Take Based on Your Brain Dump Below

☐ _____ ☐ _____

☐ _____ ☐ _____

☐ _____ ☐ _____

☐ _____ ☐ _____

☐ _____ ☐ _____

☐ _____ ☐ _____

☐ _____ ☐ _____

☐ _____ ☐ _____

☐ _____ ☐ _____

☐ _____ ☐ _____

☐ _____ ☐ _____

☐ _____ ☐ _____

Brain Dump Exercise Sheets

Faith

Fellowship

Finances

Feelings

Fitness

Brain Dump Exercise Sheets

Faith   Fellowship   Finances   Feelings   Fitness

Do This Now: Note the Actions You Can Take Based on Your Brain Dump Below

☐   ☐ _____

☐   ☐ _____

☐   ☐ _____

☐   ☐ _____

☐   ☐ _____

☐   ☐ _____

☐   ☐ _____

☐   ☐ _____

☐   ☐ _____

☐   ☐ _____

☐   ☐ _____

☐   ☐

1-PAGE ACCOUNTABILITY
WORKSHEETS

About the 1-Page Accountability Sheets

The 1-Page Accountability sheet is essentially your personal tool to help you set up a consistency system. Since being consistent is not necessarily the easiest thing to do when you get started on something or have a new goal you'd like to reach, it doesn't necessarily have to be the hardest thing either.

In short, using the 1-Page Accountability sheet allows you to easily assess and notice what actions you're taking specifically that's keeping you from being as consistent as you'd like to be. Along with this you, also have a chance to plug the holes in your execution that are draining the vital energy you need to be more reliable and consistent in the areas that matter.

How to use it:

1. Set aside 5 mins at the end of each week to go over the accountability checklist

2. When you go over the sheet, set your alarm for 5 mins as you review your week

3. Have your Intentions and Outcomes sheet on hand to note what actions you'll take to stay consistent in the week ahead

4. If you have a coach, text/call them to book a call if you're stuck for more than 2-3 weeks on a step you're taking to reach your goal

1-Page Accountability Exercise Sheet

Circle Kingdom Focus:

Faith

Fellowship

Finances

Feelings

Fitness

Week 1 Progress Steps	Week 2 Progress Steps
☐ iComplete Weekly Review Quiz (Score: _.__)	☐ iComplete Weekly Review Quiz (Score: _.__)
☐ iAdjust Action Steps to Improve My Satisfaction Level	☐ iAdjust Action Steps to Improve My Satisfaction Level
☐ iUpdate Weekly Intentions & Outcomes	☐ iUpdate Weekly Intentions & Outcomes
☐ iUpdate 3-Week Look-Ahead™	☐ iUpdate 3-Week Look-Ahead™
☐ iComplete Coaching Call (as needed)	☐ iComplete Coaching Call (as needed)
Week 3 Progress Steps	**Week 4 Progress Steps**
☐ iComplete Weekly Review Quiz (Score: _.__)	☐ iComplete Weekly Review Quiz (Score: _.__)
☐ iAdjust Action Steps to Improve My Satisfaction Level	☐ iAdjust Action Steps to Improve My Satisfaction Level
☐ iUpdate Weekly Intentions & Outcomes	☐ iUpdate Weekly Intentions & Outcomes
☐ iUpdate 3-Week Look-Ahead™	☐ iUpdate 3-Week Look-Ahead™
☐ iComplete Coaching Call (as needed)	☐ iComplete Coaching Call (as needed)
Week 5 Progress Steps (If Applicable)	**Notes and Comments**
☐ iComplete Weekly Review Quiz (Score: _.__)	☐ ....
☐ iAdjust Action Steps to Improve My Satisfaction Level	☐ ....
☐ iUpdate Weekly Intentions & Outcomes	☐ ....
☐ iUpdate 3-Week Look-Ahead™	☐ ....
☐ iComplete Coaching Call (as needed)	☐ ....

DAILY TIME & TASK
SHEETS

About the Daily Time & Task Sheets

One of the typical challenges of using a regular planner from an office supply store is not having enough space in sections to write out what you have to get done for the day by the hour.

The Daily Time & Task sheets are designed to give you daily breathing room if you've ever found yourself having to squeeze your written plans into small spaces on a regular planner. With plenty of space to write and set up your day to win, you're able to see and think clearer about your day and make changes as needed without it being too big a deal because you can see exactly where to move things if plans change. After using this sheet, you'll wonder why not all planners have pages like this.

How to use it:

1. Set aside 5-15 mins at the end of the day to go over your Daily Time & Task sheet

2. Block out sections for the most time consuming parts of the day i.e. sleep, travel, work, self care or family time

3. Use the time remaining for Daily Intentions and Outcomes sheet tasks for your most urgent and needed tasks

	AM	Daily Intentions & Outcomes	PM	Daily Intentions & Outcomes
Date		
12 AM / PM		
1 AM / PM		
2 AM / PM		
3 AM / PM		
4 AM / PM		
5 AM / PM		
6 AM / PM		
7 AM / PM		
8 AM / PM		
9 AM / PM		
10 AM / PM		
11 AM / PM		
Notes		

	AM | Daily Intentions & Outcomes	PM | Daily Intentions & Outcomes
Date		
12 AM / PM		
1 AM / PM		
2 AM / PM		
3 AM / PM		
4 AM / PM		
5 AM / PM		
6 AM / PM		
7 AM / PM		
8 AM / PM		
9 AM / PM		
10 AM / PM		
11 AM / PM		
Notes		

	AM | Daily Intentions & Outcomes	PM | Daily Intentions & Outcomes
Date		
12 AM / PM		
1 AM / PM		
2 AM / PM		
3 AM / PM		
4 AM / PM		
5 AM / PM		
6 AM / PM		
7 AM / PM		
8 AM / PM		
9 AM / PM		
10 AM / PM		
11 AM / PM		
Notes		

	AM	Daily Intentions & Outcomes	PM	Daily Intentions & Outcomes
Date		
12 AM / PM		
1 AM / PM		
2 AM / PM		
3 AM / PM		
4 AM / PM		
5 AM / PM		
6 AM / PM		
7 AM / PM		
8 AM / PM		
9 AM / PM		
10 AM / PM		
11 AM / PM		
Notes		

	AM | Daily Intentions & Outcomes	PM | Daily Intentions & Outcomes
Date		
12 AM / PM		
1 AM / PM		
2 AM / PM		
3 AM / PM		
4 AM / PM		
5 AM / PM		
6 AM / PM		
7 AM / PM		
8 AM / PM		
9 AM / PM		
10 AM / PM		
11 AM / PM		
Notes		

	AM	Daily Intentions & Outcomes	PM	Daily Intentions & Outcomes
Date		
12 AM / PM		
1 AM / PM		
2 AM / PM		
3 AM / PM		
4 AM / PM		
5 AM / PM		
6 AM / PM		
7 AM / PM		
8 AM / PM		
9 AM / PM		
10 AM / PM		
11 AM / PM		
Notes		

	AM	Daily Intentions & Outcomes	PM	Daily Intentions & Outcomes
Date		
12 AM / PM		
1 AM / PM		
2 AM / PM		
3 AM / PM		
4 AM / PM		
5 AM / PM		
6 AM / PM		
7 AM / PM		
8 AM / PM		
9 AM / PM		
10 AM / PM		
11 AM / PM		
Notes		

FINAL WORDS: WATCHING YOUR MOUTH

Hey! Watch your language! Or watch what you say. You've heard that before. I confess that I'm not always conscious of what's coming out of my mouth. And by default, I am not always conscious of my language. I'm not talking about swearing. I'm talking about monitoring my thoughts so that what I say is a match for the future and vision that I have for myself, my life or a project at hand.

Complaining - It seems today that if you're not complaining about something – the weather, the government, your kids, the bills etc., you're weird and you're not normal. But that's where we lose BIG. Complaining does one thing – highlights what you don't like, and attracts more of it by inviting other unhappy souls to you to complain with. That's called misery loving company. Stop complaining about anything in your especially time.

So, I've created a list of words to remember so that whatever you have to say or do about time is empowers you.

Language is everything. So, here are some words to add to your vocabulary as you begin your 24 Hour Blueprint journey.

✓ **Capture** – Did what you thought or what was said that you want to recall get written down in a reliable place? This is called capture or capturing. You can call it the capture-recall method.

✓ **Schedule** – Is the action required to honor that thought you captured scheduled? Is there a time and place you've noted that you'll be taking action?

✓ **Not Scheduled** – If you haven't put a task on your calendar, it's <u>not scheduled</u> and likely will not get done or get done with the level of intensity required for satisfaction and fulfillment.

✓ **Never Scheduled** – Sometimes it feels good to say, "I'm going to do this…" to a grand idea, but after review you realize you said yes to something that you can wait another lifetime to handle. So, it's okay to have a place for activities that you'll never schedule. Examples are taking the time to catch up on all the movies or TV seasons of Mad Men you'd promised yourself you'd see. Travel plans to remote parts of the earth also fall into this category.

✓ **By When…** – When people make promises to you, feel free to ask "By when?" as in, "By when should I be expecting your phone call or email or proposal?" This holds you accountable to not being a "yes" person who tolerates broken promises and unfulfilled expectations. If it's important enough, get a "by when".

✓ **Unavailable** - Given how apologetic we are about being late, missing meetings or pretending that we're interested in something only to be unresponsive to repeat invitations, it's important to identify what you're honestly available for. Just because there's time on the calendar doesn't mean you're available. Feel free to tell people, "I'm unavailable." You're availability is a function of being willing to accommodate or participate in an activity that's aligned with your 5 kingdoms. If it's not aligned with any of your 5 Kingdom intentions – you're unavailable. Be sure to communicate this to those who are involved with you on any projects or business.

REFERENCES & RECOMMENDATIONS

There's so much I've learned and unlearned over these past decade of life that has inspired the courage required to come this far and share this program with you. And it's hard to pin-point exactly where some of the individual concepts came from – because there's no one and only source that can take all the credit. Some of them are ancient and some are modernized from our repackaging of ideas in books, workshops and trainings.

One of the things that I have found helpful from time to time is tracking what resources in the form of videos or films I've watched, books or articles I've read and workshops that I've participated in which have been paradigm-shifting. Below are a few of the resources that I suggest and recommend you read, engage with, participate in or listen to in order to deepen your convictions about adapting the 24 Hour Blueprint model for your life.

Books
- Power Vs. Force, by Dr. David Hawkins
- The Power of Infinite Love and Gratitude, by Dr. Darren Weissman
- The Power of Habit, by Charles Duhigg
- The War of Art, by Steven Pressfield
- Care of the Soul, by Thomas Moore

For more references, visit **https://buihemadu.com/Favorite-books**

Films
- *Euphoria* by Lee Boot
- *Connected* by Tiffany Shlain

Programs/Trainings
- Landmark Worldwide's Curriculum for Living
- Mission Control's Trainings & Workshops
- Wright Institute's MORE Life Training
- Mankind Project's New Warrior Training Adventure

Thought Leaders & Mentors
- Michael Meade, Storyteller
- Dr. David Hawkins, Researcher and Scientist
- Joseph Campbell, Mythologist
- Werner Erhard, Transformational Leader
- Yuri Elkaim, Founder of Healthpreneur®

***Please note,** the list above is in no way exhaustive, but rather a sampling of the works that have inspired some of my work and research on this topic. There are tons more that I could list, but this is a good start.

STAYING IN TOUCH: iMISS YOU ALREADY

In closing, I love what I do. More than that, I love the people I do it for and serve – that includes YOU. If you've received great value from this and want more … Let's stay in touch – Start by becoming a member of the 24 Hour Blueprint tribe at **www.tribe.24hourblueprint.com**.

Can also email or call me. My contact information is below.

Email: **buihe@buihemadu.com**

Facebook: **http://www.facebook.com/BuiheMaduco**

Call/Text: 312-869-4196

Reminder: If you haven't already scheduled a coaching call or applied for an upcoming program, you can do so now before the next program fills up. And have Start below:

www.coaching.24hourblueprint.com

Apply For Coaching Here